The Voice of the Silenced
by Catie Cartwright

"The past should never be forgotten, however it should not be allowed to control our future, for we all have something to look forward to, and that is tomorrow."

- T. Faith Turner

Prologue:

I would like to be sure that readers are aware that some names have been changed to protect certain individuals and that there are countless memories not on these pages due to the fact that I simply told my own story, what I experienced to some degree, how I felt, and how I lived through it.

I also want readers to know that these words were put on paper as an act of healing and moving on; when I was finished friends read it, thought it was really positive, and seemed to take something good from it, therefore the only reason this book was published.

Please take all of the good that you can from this book, and leave all of the negativity inside when you are finished.

Perhaps you are carrying around an unnecessary burden as well, and I pray that if so the Lord touches you through me and this book in your hands and helps you to heal.

Thank you for taking the time to read my story...

We pray for stronger faith, for a forgiving heart, and love that can move mountains, yet when we come to the mountains we often ask to be removed from our situation, not realizing that we are contradicting our very own requests.

Dear soul, you must realize that to have faith that never wavers we must walk through fire.
To have a forgiving heart we must have the unforgivable happen to us, and for love that is undying and pure we must first come to that mountain where only a heart and soul that is fully entwined with the Lord can allow us the strength to move….

How often we forget that while crossing a bridge that could fall at any moment is when we fully learn to trust in the Lord's hand, and by that our faith grows to its full extent as he had planned.

- Catie Cartwright

1.

The day started out as any other 'dentist day' would have. Wake up at six a.m., shower, then eat a fast breakfast where Dad would insist that my older sister and I drink this horrible orange drink called tang.
He said it was healthy, yet we thought it tasted just awful, but we drank it anyway.

Mom and Dad were still not getting along and things were tense, as they had been since Mom had gotten sick. She would lie on the bathroom floor and cry and cry. She suffered from hives almost daily as well.

The church we went to said she was "letting the devil possess her mind."
I didn't know, but my Mom was hurting and that scared me, so I would sit on the bathroom floor for hours with her and just play silently with my toys.

I was nine then, and my sister Angel was fifteen.
Our lives at that point in time consisted of going to church, working on the farm, and being home schooled.

We went to church on Sundays, Wednesdays, and Fridays. Our church was not very big at all and it was really quite peculiar I thought.

The pastor Adrian, and his wife Joan owned a lot of land in Oldtown, Maryland which they called "The Lord's Farm".

It was a farm, that part was true, and the farm was huge; it had enough room to have several houses on it without even being close to hearing distance from the other.

They lived here on the farm, somewhat like the Amish, as in they ate and were clothed off the fruits of the crops and the profits of their labor.
They also made some money from selling vegetables, fruits, hand-made

crafts, clothes, and pies, cookies, etc at farmers markets.

2.

The first memory I have is of Valley Street, and I don't remember much about there, I was a baby the whole time we were there.

Fast forward about two years; me, my sister, Mom and Dad have moved to a trailer park in Fort Ashby, West Virginia.

On the weekends we usually go to my grandma's (my mom's mother).
Life was good, we made friends with the neighbor kids Jason and Strett.
Mom and Dad became friends with

their parents as well, and they invited us to their church.

We went, it was small, maybe three or four families and a few single people; had worship in a living room, sang and played instruments, in addition to a sermon, and then a meal.
It was pretty fun at first and the food was always delicious; we made some friends and so did Mom and Dad.

Before you knew it, we were becoming a part of a sick and twisted family united together by a common yearning to please the Lord how they perceived to be right.

Mom and Dad built a house in Greenspring and soon we moved in. I was three at this time and Angel nine. As we settled in I started my first schooling as a homeschooler, and Angel was being pulled out of her public school.

Everyone in the church home schooled their kids; that's what they thought they were supposed to do because "the world is an evil place and they should protect their children from such things."

Things changed slowly more and more. Girls couldn't wear pants, jeans or shorts but had to wear skirts or dresses. Little by little we saw outside friends and family less and less.

By the time I was six or seven we had stopped seeing my outside family altogether.

When I say outside I mean people that were not members of our church.

"The church was our family, and we were to act that way" Joan had told me.

One hot summer day, a lot of the women were working in the garden down the road from the farmhouse, near one of the other original houses on the property.

I was near the end of a row and not especially close to anyone except for

Joan.

I made a small comment about my Pap, and how much I missed him.

Immediately, my comment was returned with:

"He isn't your grandfather, we are your family now."

She then stated that Adrian could be a grandfather to me now.

Confused, hurt, and just as much knowing any questions would be considered 'back-talk' I remained silent.

3.

I missed my Ma, (maternal great grandmother) my Grandmother, and my Pap the most.
My Ma was a tiny little English WWII bride and I loved her dearly.

At least two years had passed that I hadn't seen her at all and we received a phone call that she was in the hospital dying.
I remember holding my doll, staring at Ma's fuzzy little face, she could see me, but she couldn't talk really, only smile slightly.

I was so heartbroken, knowing what time I had missed, and knowing that this was the very last time I would ever see her alive again.

At two a.m. that night I woke suddenly, sitting straight up in bed for a moment or so.

As I sat there in the dark the phone rang. I could hear Mom answering and talking softly.

She was dead. Ma had passed on. It was the spring of 1998.

We weren't allowed to go to her viewing or funeral, "She wasn't of

God" according to the church, so Mom ran in two roses (plastic, so they would never wither) from my sister and I to her casket and laid them in with something of her own and ran back out.

Every time I go to a funeral home I always think of this.

How can I not?
As soon as I walk in they always have a basket or two of the caramel Werther's Originals candies by where you sign your name in the guest book.
These were my Ma's favorites and she would always give them to me.
I always take one and as I eat it the memories of her flood back and I can

feel her warmth against my face giving me a hug and squeezing me lovingly.

This is when Mom really started to get sick.
Other things had happened as well, her Dad (my Pap) had gotten quite sick not long before Ma died.
I was too young to know this then, but he got very ill and forgot a lot of things for a small time and Joan told Mom that she would pay for his soul if he died because she was unable to persuade him to become a member of the church and repent.

4.

When Mom finally told the people at church that she was sick, they said it was "all in her head, and she was of the devil and letting him control her."

I don't think Dad even knew what to do, Mom was so depressed and sick all of the time; she had anxiety and panic attacks, she also suffered from stress induced hives nearly daily.
She clearly needed help, but I didn't know how or what to do, just like Dad.

Eventually things got so bad Mom wouldn't even ride in a car anymore, she was too scared for a period of time.

She stayed home from church, and apparently that wasn't too good of an idea because the next time she did go Joan and Adrian asked her to talk to them in private.

When they came out, Mom was upset, and crying, and Dad was really confused looking.
Adrian and Joan? Cold as ice and quiet. They had just kicked my Mom out of the church; I found out a little bit later.

Out of our church, our family, and just like that they all turned their backs on her.

Our family had just thrown my mother out, telling her to never come back.
Told her that she was evil and would burn in hell forever and there was no hope for her.
She would always be this way.

Mom and Dad had never ever fought in front of us, so what happened next really shocked us girls.
All of a sudden, everything was different, it wasn't Mom and Dad, it was suddenly Mom 'or' Dad.
I'm pretty sure that crumbled everything right there that I ever believed about love and trust.

I had been broken quickly as a child upon joining the church, and pain was no stranger to me, in fact you could say he was so close that at times he was a shadow, something I could never get away from.

I knew what it was like very young to know I had no one to truly talk to because if what I said was bad or worse than something they had done, whoever I talked to would just run and tell either Mom or the pastor and his wife.
I knew what it felt like at a young age to want God to take everything away, and take me up to him.

5.

After this, things fell like dominoes.

Mom was forced to move out of our
home, the locks were changed on her,
and the doctrine of the church had an
even stronger hold on my Father than
ever before.

Let's talk about my Dad for just a
minute.
He was born to a very young, beautiful
lady who was approximately sixteen
years old.
His Dad had left upon hearing of the

pregnancy and never came around after he was born.

His younger brother Keese was born not too long after.
When my Dad was two his mom was hitch hiking and was hit by a vehicle and killed.
Her mother (Dad's grandmother) tried to adopt both boys out but only successfully adopted out Keese and raised my Dad until he was fifteen or sixteen, at which time he moved out with Mom because of Angel being born.

My Father never met his father until I

was about six or seven I'd say.
We were all at home on a cool evening,
no snow, but I think it was winter.
Anyhow, I was downstairs and
someone pulled up the driveway. I
opened the basement door not thinking
anything odd was about to happen.

The man I saw in front of me was
almost a replica of my Dad, but older.
I ran upstairs and told Dad that I think
maybe his dad or someone that looked
just like him was at the door.

They talked for a long time and then he
left. My Dad was in his early thirties
that night.

Dad filed for divorce in October 2000.
When Mom was at the house they
fought constantly, physically and orally,
so I stayed out of the way a lot.
I would sit under my sister's desk in her
bedroom a lot, writing in my little
spiral notebook about everything
happening around me.

My life officially had fallen apart.

6.

So that brings us back to the beginning
of part one…to dentist day.
Myself, my sister and my Dad piled
into his truck and headed to the dentist,
leaving Mom at home crying as usual.
Everything went smooth and soon we
came home ready to get on with the rest
of the day.
Dad tells us out of the blue to pack
some bags because we would be
staying down at the farmhouse on the
farm for the next few days.

Confused, but knowing we had no
choice but to obey, we packed quickly

and quietly.

We entertained ourselves quietly in the living room while Mom and Dad screamed and fought in the basement. We couldn't see downstairs, only hear. I heard the basement door slam, and Dad came running up the stairs.

"Angel! Get the truck! Quick! I'll meet you girls down the driveway by the pond!" he yelled.

Nervously we grabbed our belongings and hopped into the truck.
Angel backed up slowly.

"Whats happening?" I whispered, softly, trying not to cry.

"I don't know" was all she mumbled.

Obediently she drove to the pond Dad.
Dad was running down the hill to meet
us. He jumped in and told her to step on
it.
"Don't turn around girls! Don't look
behind us!" He was hollering.

I couldn't listen, I had to know why I
shouldn't look, I had to see.

I turned and peeked over the seat and
out the back window, and that's when I
saw her - Mom was crying, screaming,
begging for us not to leave her,
barefoot running on the gravel road,
feet bleeding.

Angel hit the brakes on instinct when
Dad yelled not to look back.
"I told you not to slow down or look!
GO!" he screamed.

I wanted to scream, to hit him. I kept
watching her chase us as Angel
fearfully followed Dad's orders.
Thats when it happened.

She fell, flat on her face, in the gravel,
and skid to a stop. And didn't move. At
all. She stayed face down.

I screamed at the top of my lungs and
since I was in the middle seat of the
truck I could just reach the brake pedal

between Angel's legs. I stomped on it with all of my might.

"I said don't stop!" Dad yelled again.

"DAD! SHE'S DEAD!" I screamed at him

"No - She's just faking! She'll get back up! She just wants you to think that." He said flippantly.

At that moment, in all of the chaos, the screaming, the truck stopped in the middle of our long driveway….
I thought that I had lost my Mom forever, just like my Ma.
She was facedown, not moving a

muscle. How could Dad let this happen?! Why did he do this to her?! Why couldn't he have just stayed with her?

As my big brown eyes filled with tears, my vision blurred, but my eyes never left her. She slowly started to move and climbed to her cut and bloodied feet, stumbling back up the driveway. I screamed that she was hurt, she needed our help.

Dad drove back up the driveway, put her in the bed of the truck, took her back to the house, and then proceeded to take us to the farm.

The drive was so long it seemed. All I could think was 'Will I ever see my Mom again? Will she be ok?'

When we got to the farm all I can remember is collapsing into someone's arms crying my eyes out, vigorously shaking from my sobs.

It hurt, like a knife in my back, this family had done this to my Mom.
I didn't understand anything that was happening. Where did my family go? Why did Joan and Adrian tell me Mom was "of the devil" and I would "go to hell if I went with her and not Dad"?

Why did they say it "was a sin to tell

Mom I loved her"? It didn't used to be.

Why were they asking why we were late, and when Dad explained that Mom fell and we took her back to the house, why did they say that we "should have left her in the ditch"? Why would they say such a thing?! They were supposed to be her family!

7.

Our church started as simply a family gathering that grew.
Friends and friends of friends started to come too, and slowly a 'fellowship' was created.

The doctrine of our beliefs was founded on the King James Version Bible, yet were in many ways taken extremely out of proportion, causing a more 'extreme doctrine' of christianity.

This extreme 'version' of christianity proved to be family fatal and dangerous, causing one to hurt the people they love in order to support something they believed held the secret to pleasing the Lord.

Dad says when we first went it just seemed 'right' - "they were reading the Bible, praising the Lord, everything about it made you believe."

Words we lived by, was what the Bible seemed to me.
I didn't really understand a lot of it, I just knew it was what I had to do or I would go to hell.
In our church, anyone was welcome,

but once you came, and if you joined…
if you ever were to leave the church
you would leave your family (if you
had one in the church) and your church
friends behind forever.

"Shunned" was a word I heard a lot.
We read verses like 2nd Corinthians
6:17 …
"come out from among them…be (you)
separate says the Lord…and I will
receive you…" And take that as,
whoever isn't a member of our church
is wrong and we can't associate with
them..family or not.

"What part hath he that believeth with
an infidel?"

- 2nd Corinthians 6:15

"Be (you) not unequally yoked together with unbelievers"
-2nd Corinthians 6:14

We stayed at the farm for about four days overnight.

While we stayed over night there we were awake at six a.m., breakfast, feed the farm animals, work in the garden, break at nine-thirty a.m., work till lunch.
Lunch and nap twelve to one, then work again till dinner at five then work till dark.

It was heavy work - five gallon buckets with cucumbers and beans and stuff are heavy when you're that young but it taught me not to complain and how to work hard - and to be strong.
I was also used to working like this, we had been doing this with Mom and my sister on the farm for years.

Those four days just seemed like an eternity. I guess because we never left.

When we finally came back home after those four days, Mom wasn't there.

8.

…My eyes opened slowly…someone was rustling around in my drawer…It was Mom!

I jumped up as if to hug her - tell her how happy I was to see her and to know she was alive - but my fear of going to hell and everything Joan and Adrian told me was too great.
I wanted to tell her I wanted to go with her - I didn't want to stay here - I didn't want her to be alone out there in the world - but I couldn't - I was too afraid, so instead I just got out of bed and

smiled at her.

She smiled and walked across the room to make up my bed.

As I watched her pull up the blankets I noticed something on her wrists and neck...
They were little cut marks...
'Oh my goodness! Mom tried to kill herself!'

"Mom - what happened?" I asked, softly taking her hand and turning it over, slowly revealing the marks.
Jerking her hand back to hide them, "Nothing, nothing, I'm just having a hard time right now thats all but I'm

fine, really I'm fine don't worry….I'm fine" she said reassuringly..

Only if she knew she wasn't reassuring anyone that day.

It seemed at this point that Dad just wanted to get away so he took advantage of teaching Angel to get her license and we took small trips often. Since it was just us (Dad, Angel and I) it was actually pretty fun and we could get away a little from the hell around us.

He often took us to work with him, (he is a mechanic, was taught mainly by my mother's dad) I enjoyed that a lot, I liked working on cars with him or helping by cleaning tools and the shop.

9.

Had I not
created my whole world,
I would certainly
have died
in other people's

- Anais Nin

Things steadily got worse as days
seemed like weeks.
Mom was never at home anymore, and
neither were we.

Dad dropped us off at the farm in the
mornings before work and picked us up
in the evenings after.
We did our schoolwork at the farm, and
when I was done I would usually do
whatever chores Joan wanted done and
then I could play in the woods.

The woods have been a magical place
for me all of my life, a place where I
could get away from any bit of reality
that was hurting or bothering me.
I could pretend to be whoever I wanted

and do whatever I wanted.

I would imagine elaborate things like the world of Narnia (before I even knew Narnia existed in the world that knows it as C.S. Lewis) because my imagination had to be that large to let me escape when I could.

The rest of the time I spent not in the woods I had to listen and focus, hear and speak the correct answers wanted to be heard by those elder than me.

The woods were a blessing from God, with the beauty of the birds, each with their own beautiful song, turtles, salamanders, and crayfish, all of the beautiful creatures.

Adorned in the beautiful array of colors,from light pink to the deepest red, the wild roses that smell so sweet, the anemone growing on the side of the rock above the creek that even I could barely climb to.

I would climb to the tops of the highest trees and sit for as long I could and enjoy the view and my bit of freedom. Wondering if I would ever get to see any more than my small world.

Wondering if my life would ever change from the way it was. Was anyone else out there in this world? Was I as alone as I felt?

I would imagine and hope that anyone at all that was from that world out there would walk down that road and talk to me.

Would I always be stuck here? Working in a field or a greenhouse, babysitting or washing dishes, weeding the beans for the ninetieth time this summer, washing produce, going to church three days a week and being home schooled, learning about half of what I should or even would like to be learning?
At least I had the woods, at least I could escape here and dream, visit my animal friends and simply be a kid.

I would usually stay in the woods as

long as possible everyday.

Not hiding, but praying a lot, and writing while sitting up on a tree branch, or maybe under my favorite pine, or my favorite rotten log on that cliff that over hung the river.

I loved these escapes more than anything and I thank God he gave them to me.

After Angel got her driver's license Dad got her a little white Honda from Adrian and Joan's son so that we could drive ourselves to the farm and back now everyday.

That thirty-five minute drive was like Heaven, we could listen to what we wanted to, or talk about whatever, but usually we just listened to music we weren't supposed to…

When we got close, Angel would click on the right hand turn signal for the drive up the farm road…I'd slide in a michael card (hymn singer) tape, and up the road to the farm we would go…. We had that thirty-five minutes at least, right?

10.

For even as I laid it on, I said, I will be near, and while she leans on me this burden will be mine, not hers

- Anonymous

Through out all of this I buried myself deeply in parts of the Bible that I did understand....

My favorite, 1st Peter 5:7 ....

"Casting all

your care upon Him, for He careth for you."

When you close your eyes,
He will smile
I close my eyes….
I tell him my worries,
all of them - because he wants them all
I open my eyes…
I have forgotten…
that which worried me…
they are in his hands
it is his work now
- Catie Cartwright

I love that: being able to say, "It is His work now" knowing that I have left everything in his hands and he is responsible for my well being and I know he will care for me if I trust him, it is his work now.

That verse also gave me comfort knowing that if I had NO ONE I would still NEVER BE ALONE.

"The Lord shall help them..deliver and save them…because they trust in Him "
-Psalms 37:40

"He will fulfill the desire of those that fear Him - He will hear their cry and will save them"
- Psalms 145:19

"The Lord will keep him in perfect
peace whose mind is stayed on
thee" (keep your mind on God and he
will keep you at peace)
- Isaiah 26:3

"And even when we lose the thing that
seems most dear? Our loss is gain - in
him we have our all" - Anonymous

My sister and I grew even closer over
the next few months.
We spent all of our time together. At
sixteen years old my sister practically
had to be the woman of the house and
cook and clean and wash clothes, and
also teach me about puberty, which she

did her best at and I thank her for I truly do.

Slowly I began to adapt to my changing body, altho I hated the fact that girls have periods - but it's a fact of life that every girl eventually gets used to.

11.

Mom and Dads divorce had now turned into a full blown custody battle.

We had already been to court several times, but this time the judge talked to my sister and I separately, away from Dad, each other and the pastor and their family. Standard questions, who I wanted to live with, was I abused or afraid, etc.

Alone, sitting with my hands clasped together in my lap nervously, across the desk from the judge, a million thoughts running through my head.

'I really miss my Mom, but Joan says
she is of the devil, Dad says she's not
Mom anymore….
whatever that means…
Mom was just sick, but no one
understands her or will help her….
what do I say? No, I'm not abused but I
can't even call my Mom and tell her I
love her?
No one at the church can do anything
unless Joan and Adrian think it's ok?
Yes I'm afraid so afraid…
I don't know how to feel…
I feel numb..
I'm done hurting..
I've built walls for those spears…but I

do have nightmares all the time…
and Joan says that's of the devil too..
Dad says Mom is the enemy like in the
book of Psalms..what does that mean
either?
o wow..I've just been sitting here
thinking..I gotta say somethin…'

"No, I am not afraid.
I love my Dad. I want to live with him.
I am not abused and I like it with Dad."

The words were rolling off my tongue,
contradicting my very thoughts.
I had not been rehearsed as what to say,
but what I should say in many different
situations had been very clearly made
known to me by Dad, Joan and Adrian.

So I said it.

Hell on earth or hell forever? I chose quickly on that.

Hearing what I said, he began to almost repeat the same question, just worded differently.

After realizing my answer was staying the same, he wrote something down and stood up.

Smiling, he thanked me and showed me out into the hall where Dad and everyone else was waiting.
I later found out that what he wrote

down was that my sister and I needed to see a therapist.

12.

Court ordered, Angel and I went to a local therapist. Angel went first, as I sat in the waiting room with Dad, staring silently at the rug on the floor.

I was irritated.
'Why did I have to be here? I wasn't crazy! Mom and Dad are the crazy ones right now!
Mom says I'm brainwashed…by Joan and Adrian…
What does that mean? Mom and Dad should be here! Not me!

Dad says if Mom gets custody she'll make me take medicine that will take God out of my heart and make me not believe in God anymore! Then I would go to hell!'

"Catie he's ready for you" the secretary interrupted my crazy hoard of thoughts and brought me back to the waiting room.

I walked into the room and looked around, it looked actually inviting, with tons of books everywhere, I love books. There was a couch, a recliner, some plants, everything reeked of relaxation and emotions.
I hated this - the fact that it was warm

and inviting in there. I wanted to speak, but I couldn't.

It made me angry…the pot had already been boiling before I walked in here and now it was just exploding over the sides of my soul.

"Hi Catie" he said gently.

"How are you? Please, make yourself at home - take a seat if you like"

He gestured towards the couch with its fluffy pillows and wooden oak feet.

"I'm fine, how are you?" I replied.

I had been raised with manners and taught how to be polite, if anything at the farm, so that was good at least.

"So, is there anything you'd like to talk about?" he asked invitingly.

"I know your going through a lot with your parents getting divorced and everything - I'm sure that's hard on you"

'Haahaa……He doesn't even know the half of the messed up story' I am thinking.

"The custody battle - I'm sure everything is very confusing for you right now"..
He drawled to a stop when he saw that I wasn't paying attention, but leafing though an old book that I had pulled from the book shelf.
I looked at him blankly when I heard his silence.

Slamming the book shut and returning it to its home on the shelf, I turned and said to him-

"You have NO IDEA what I am going through and even if I told you I bet you wouldn't believe me! It's all so crazy right now, and even if you did, you wouldn't understand, so don't waste our time trying to get me to talk about my messed up life, can we just sit here silently for as long as I have to be back here?"

I had never sounded so mean, bitter, or harsh in my life; I barely even recognized the voice I heard. I sat down and finished speaking-

"Please sir, I don't need yet another person telling me how to live and what to think or do."

"You seem a bit shut down, are you sure you don't want to talk about it?… About anything at all?" He inquired gently.

"When can I leave?" I responded quietly.

He smiled and rose, walking to the door "Ladies first." He motioned.

13.

The next few weeks were exhausting.
Farm, school, lawyers, court, church,
home, it seemed like a lot to handle;
between body changes and school, that
should be enough right?
No, there was so much more..I taught
myself a lot of my schoolwork after
fourth grade.
By that point I had answer books to
check my own work with.
I cheated a lot at math, so much that I
failed my s.a.t. on math one year. I
studied the answer book to retake the
s.a.t and somehow I passed, but I really

didn't learn anything in depth with math at all.

Every time we had a court date, Adrian and Joan and their two daughters Haley and Amber always went with my Dad or met us there.
I didn't really understand why they were there, and I didn't feel like it was their place to be there.

Things were so bad because of them, they divided the room, as in "She wasn't our Mom over there crying, begging to give us a hug and see us, that was the devil in her trying to suck me to hell" making it clear in my head that even looking at her for too long would be willingly putting one foot in hell's gate.

Dad, his lawyer and The Lord's Farm presented a case against Mom based on her mental stability at that point in time in efforts to win custody for my Father.

Since we had no opinion in it (because we didn't want to go to hell) Dad eventually was granted custody and Mom had visitation rights, every Wednesday from seven p.m. to nine p.m. and every other weekend.
In other words, the extreme doctrine of our church had successfully torn yet another loving family to shreds, leaving now only crushed hearts and broken

promises in its wake.

The day that happened in court I will never forget.

14.

Mom and Dad both took the stand, my Grandma,and Mom's Dad (they were divorced) were there, and some really big tall bearded man on Mom's side.

All of Mom's side were lined up on the bench outside of the courtrooms as we walked into the hallway.
As soon as Mom saw us girls her eyes lit up and she jumped up and ran over to hug us.
Immediately, before she could even get to us, Joan, her family and Dad formed a circle around us, blocking us from our

Mother.

Mom went crazy, for good reason.

"I just want to hug my daughters! You can't do this to me! You can't keep them from me like this!" she yelled.

"You're doing this to yourself! You have strayed from God! This is why this is all happening to you!" Joan returned her shouts.

The fury rose in Mom's eyes, her dark browns turning black as night, it seemed as if she could almost spit fire.

"You all have brainwashed my girls to hate me! Duane I can't believe you would let this happen!"

'There's that brainwashed word again -

really wish I knew what that meant'…
I thought..Mom was screaming..the
next thing I knew the bailiff was
grabbing Mom, she was kicking,
punching, screaming…

Another came to help, they pulled her
into a room and I didn't see her again
until inside the courtroom.

Thus began the packing and unpacking,
back and forth between Mom and Dad.
Visitation was spent at our Grandma's
house with her husband (Mom's
stepdad) George, and Mom.

It was awkward. Angel and I were
outside as much as possible, or alone in

our room.

We socialized as little as possible, because when we did talk, a lot of what they wanted to talk about was how bad the church and Dad was, and of course we didn't want to hear that.

When we went home, it was the same way, all they wanted to talk about was Mom, what did she say to you, how terrible she was, etc.

Honestly, I was miserable everywhere.

15.

The doctrine that had torn our family apart I now believe is ungodly and unrealistic.

When I was little it didn't really matter if I really believed it or not, it was all I knew, I didn't know there was a whole world out there full of freedom, so really what was I to believe?

As things were painful, more than not, I folded even more into myself. I quieted, a lot, spent a lot more time alone than with anyone, and wrote a lot more also.

I didn't really understand a lot of what was taught at church, because we said we believed in the Bible, but in the Bible it talks about a God who loves all and forgive anyone, were supposed to be like him, or do our best, yet we only saw the same people every day, we didn't talk to anyone else.

How do you let a light shine if you hide it?

I never voiced any of my opinions, I learned fast when to know your wasting our breath.
At a very young age I picked up a mature sense to be quiet, take it all in,

and ponder the truth. Sometimes I
didn't know the truth, but I felt that I'd
one day know if I needed to.

As a child it seems you're so busy with
life; school, chores, playing, eating,
everything a child does; that you can
ignore pain, it hits you and you get
distracted and forget moments later, but
having Mom ripped away from me
without so much as a goodbye hug was
really hard for me to handle.

I called out to God for strength, to
never show that I was afraid or hurting,
to continue on until he directed me
elsewhere.

"God's greatest gifts come through great pain."
- Anonymous

"Children..obey your parents in all things..." (Colossians 3:20-21)

I now think that first, we must realize who our true parents our, the Lord. In the very next verse it states:

"Fathers, provoke not your children to anger…do not discourage them.."

We were told to listen, and that's what we did. I would have listened to my parents over anyone, but it's very

confusing, when for nine years you listen to your Mother, then all of a sudden she is a bad person.
Do I still listen to her?

16.

September 11, 2001. It was my
eleventh birthday. It was beautiful,
clearer than freshly cleaned window
panes, and not hot, but perfect.

I was dropped off at Adrian and Joan's
son's house to help with watching and
homeschooling their five children.

We were all sitting around the dining
room table doing schoolwork when the
phone rang.
It was Joan and Adrian's son from work
(he was a nurse at the hospital, as it was

the custom in the church that the man be the breadwinner and the woman take care of the home and children) he said a plane had crashed into the pentagon and that two planes had crashed into the world trade center twin towers.

What was the pentagon? Or the twin towers? We hadn't had cable since I was probably two or three (or had we ever had cable? I wasn't really that sure) we didn't even own a television at this point; I didn't know anyone who did.

His wife said it was a terrorist attack..once again what is that? "People from other countries are hijacking planes and flying them into important government buildings." She explained.

'Nice, on my birthday' I thought..

I didn't realize until the next day when I saw the newspaper how horrific that terrorist attack had been, or how many people had died horrible painful deaths for such a terrible reason.

Around this time a lot of our belongings were gotten rid of them, I'm still not sure where they all ended up but it was a whole trailer load full of items like books, toys, etc of both mine and Angel's.

Ninety percent of the items that we had

from when we were little, anything and everything we had was gotten rid of. We were not asked about any of it; but then again, we were just kids that had to listen.

That winter, our visits with Mom were either spent with our cousins that we met that lived by our Grandma's or the neighbors the Markers.
They opened their home to us and made us feel welcome any time we were at our Grandma's and needed a place to go to get away from it all.

My cousin Jacob was my age and his younger brother Jeremy was about three years younger.

It was the first time I could ever remember I had someone my same age to play with. All of my other friends had always been older or years younger.

We went sledding and exploring, we had a lot of fun. It was a great escape from the hell around us. That winter in itself was actually pretty good, up until one night upon returning home from visitation.

17.

"Your entire world will turn into a
battlefield tonight.."
-Disturbed

The drive was normal but after we got inside the house Dad said he needed to talk to us about something important. He sat us down in the living room:

"Ok" he started slowly,
"I know this is going to be a huge shock to you girls but I need to tell you that Haley and I are going to get married."

'Haley is Joan and Adrian's daughter, youngest daughter, maybe 21! She was Angel's friend! They had sleepovers together in this very house! As friends - not as my Dad's girlfriend!'
My mind was turning so fast - I screamed:

"Dad! How could you? I hate you for this! How could you do this?!"

I ran down the hall to my room, slamming and locking the door behind me and sliding to the floor, back against the door, knees to my chest; screaming in my head to God that this was more than I could take.

"Catie, Haley is coming over soon and when she does you had better come downstairs and welcome her into our family!" Dad yelled down the hall…

"NEVER! I HATE THIS! I WONT DO IT!"
I screamed back through the door..

'What about Mom? We would really never be a family again?! What was going to happen now?

Would Haley just move into Mom and Dad's old room with Dad? And why her? She's like an older sister…not a stepmom…wow..

I was going to have a stepmom..

NO! I DONT WANT ONE! I DONT NEED ONE!'

knock knock

a soft tapping on the door interrupted my racing thoughts.

"Let me in - it's just me." Angel was whispering softly through the door...

I let her in and together we sat on my

blue rug on the floor.

"Are you gonna talk to her Angel?" I ask.

"Are you?" She returns the question.

"I don't know…" I responded quietly. I didn't know..I didn't want to I knew that..it seemed really way too fast for this..but I knew I'd get in trouble if I didn't do it…so I really didn't have a choice..

or a voice in this case..or…ever.

"Maybe we should just do it and get it over with and not get in trouble." Angel says.

"I don't want to…" I said softly.

"Me neither, really." She replied.

Our hearts sank as we sat together..unsure of what would happen in our future...even more unsure than yesterday..lights were coming up the driveway slowly..

"It's her" I say.

Angel took my hand…

"Let's go, let's do this together."

Dad and Haley were already seated together downstairs by the time we came down. I walked over and sat on the rock mantel by the wood stove.

"Angel, Catie," Dad said, taking Haley's hand, "We are in love, and after much prayer and talking it over with Joan and Adrian, we've decided to get married."

'Yup - you were just done with Mom so you kicked her to the curb and you wanted someone else and Haley was just there, of course you want her' thoughts were streaming through my head - always too fast for me to even keep up - Haley said something about her marrying Dad was not meaning she was taking the place of Mom but she would love us like her own..

"Ok well thats nice - gnyt everybody" I really needed to go to bed…
I cried myself to sleep that night...I

really missed Mom.

18.

Now that Dad was marrying Haley, we would be moving to the farm into a farmhouse.

'Goodbye tree house…tire swing..our dog Joe's grave…my bedroom…my house…'

The farmhouse was really old and it needed a lot of work done before we could move into it. The church got together to repair and redo the entire house.

No one but me, Angel, Haley, her sister

Amber, and her parents knew at this time that they were engaged.

I was one of those to work on the house every day - ripping down old wallpaper - sanding, painting, staining, paneling; made for a long days work.

When I wasn't working on the house I was doing schoolwork in Haley's room at her house…ironic?

No…haha…

I said it was quieter up there but really I had to get to the bottom of this; I had to know, did Dad cheat on Mom?

So little by little I tore her room apart searching everywhere, every nook and cranny, every crack, book, drawer - I read about her life up until the day that Dad had told her he loved her, and that was about a month before Dad had told us about it.

So I guess he didn't, but now I was even more confused, how can you love someone and be married to them for over sixteen years, and then just get a divorce and fall in love the first time you turn around?

19.

Over the next week or two things changed even more drastically. Angel was old enough now to either stay with us or go live elsewhere by herself.

Over the earlier months she had gotten closer to the Markers and they offered her a place to live until she could get out on her own.

She accepted.

Not Dad, not Haley, not anyone did anything to change her mind!

Instead, Joan told her to contact every member of the church and tell them she was turning her back on all of them. Although every response she got was different, a few were encouraging and helped her find more of the strength that she needed that day.

Some even told her she was doing the right thing. Although I never told her anything except that I loved her and I'd miss her, and she'd be ok, I knew she was doing the right thing too.

I then walked out of the farmhouse and across the stream to my favorite pine and sat under it and watched as she left.

I was trying not to be overwhelmed, my

best friend was leaving - I had Strett
but still, he was a boy and nothing like
Angel!

What was I going to do? Who would I
talk to when I really needed someone
now?

I had no one left..only God.

She drove home and packed her things,
and Dad dropped her and her suitcase
off at the Markers and then came and
got me from the farm.
That night was an awful blur,

I don't clearly remember much after
that point of this night.

It was like I wasn't even there, and I don't want to remember the few things that I do about that night.

20.

Months passed, we had sold our house, moved, and I'd now kind of settled into the new place. I liked the idea of new surroundings to explore, I had always loved exploring.

Haley was not home that often during this time, She'd go to her Mom's or somewhere, I'm not too sure, I didn't really care, I loved the freedom of being home alone.

I'd turn on all the radios in the house almost as loud as they'd go on a rock channel-Metallica, Tom Petty, Pantera,

I had never heard any of it before and it was awesome! There was such good music to be heard!

I loved the deep strain of the rock sound, the heaviness of a metal song when it would play, as if they were taking the music straight from my soul. As if they knew how my pain felt and had found a way to let it out and turn it into that beautiful sounding music called metal.

I listened to everything the radio would play when I was alone.

I loved hearing the drums on the radio in heavier songs. I would turn up all the radios on the same channel as loud as they would go and open the windows. Then I would crawl out onto the porch

roof and listen and enjoy myself.
Myself and my new found friend,
music.

I wrote letters to Angel during this
time.
Her life was only starting, everything
was all new to her, and would be for a
long time. She had to get a car, a job,
and would actually have a normal (or
somewhat normal) real life.

Every day was a new experience for
her. I was happy for her. She deserved
to have fun and be a teenager.
Her responsibilities had gone from
taking care of Dad and I to taking care
of only herself.

That summer I spent a lot of time riding my bike and playing with Strett, who was my neighbor now up the hill. They had moved down here about a year earlier.

Things seemed brighter, I could smell something coming in the air..I couldn't tell what..but something was coming…

21.

It was my weekend with Mom, Saturday afternoon, August 16, 2003, to be exact, when I got a phone call from Dad.

He told me that last Sunday they had made it open at church about him and Haley and a lot of people hadn't taken it that well.
A lot of the women had been friends with Mom so I understood what their issue was, so that part I was already waiting on, but what he said next made me almost drop the phone.

He said that the next day all the women had talked to Joan, coming forward with how they felt about everything for the past many years, how they felt about the doctrine and Joan herself. They wanted out - they'd had enough of the evil control.

By that night the entire church had broken, people were going to be moving, the farm would be selling, and the Lord's Farm was...

…no…more...

I rushed Dad off of the phone so I could go for a walk and talk to God and thank him, thank him for the end of the hell that had been my life.

I had to celebrate!

I remember laughing, crying, this was the best day of my life!

Fourteen years later, this still takes the trophy for the best day of my life, for me, it was the day that I slowly began MY life.

It was as if a huge black cloud had lifted from over me - and it was real! I wasn't dreaming!

I would never go to church again with them! I would never have to listen to them again! I was free!

When I got home Dad sat and talked to me and told me how he felt like his eyes had been opened to all the wrong ways he had been living and leading his family in.

He apologized for everything that had ever happened and asked for my forgiveness.

I forgave him. I understood no one is perfect and people make mistakes.

Some good had come from it.
I had an amazing faith in the Lord.
I knew how to work hard, and I also now knew how to appreciate all of the many things that I would experience that I had so far missed out on.

I believe that our healing process didn't

really complete though, until he read this.

He never knew how much I had hurt as a child. I never showed it, but I needed him to know that I wasn't a rock on the inside, I was a normal child with hurts and fears and I needed him to see what it was that he actually apologized for those years ago.

On a side note I would like to clarify that my relationship with my Father is amazing.
I can talk to him about anything, I know he is there for me if I need him, I know that he loves me no matter what, and I enjoy every minute that I am able

to spend with him.

A little word to readers…is there something that someone has done that adversely affected you and even though they apologized they don't know *how* it affected you?
Tell them..talk it out..cry it out..trust me..if they can be open and willing to hear it, it will help in the long run.

22.

Dad was still marrying Haley but I didn't care at this point; things were going to be totally different now. Joan and Adrian had lost the loyalty of their church family forever.

After that, the farm property, animals, and equipment were auctioned off. Dad and Haley had to move too, and I decided to move in with Mom and a man whom she had married named Galen. (He was the big bearded man I saw a long time ago at that court date.)

They had a house with a pond and

some goats, it was a beautiful place.

Soon enough I was situated in yet another new place to live, and I liked it here a lot.

By now Angel had also moved in with Mom - life was so good at the time!

That winter we had the holidays with the family for the first time that *I* could *ever* remember.

It had been since before I was five or six.

My Dad and Haley had a baby boy a year later. I had always hoped and prayed for a little brother and in a strange way my prayers had been answered.

I was one of the happiest girls alive that day; me and my sister drove down to the hospital to see him. He was perfect! I was so excited!

23.

Up to this point I'd been home schooled my entire life, and I knew one person besides my cousin who was around my age and that was Strett - who I didn't really talk to anymore because they had moved and he wasn't really allowed to contact me.

I was curious, I wanted to meet people, make friends, see what it was like out there.

That fall I started ninth grade. In a three floor school with about four hundred students, probably more.

I didn't realize how sheltered I had been my entire life until this point.

I knew nothing of the world today, the little I did know wasn't enough to make me seem like just a regular kid.

Going to school was very intimidating. My first day I realized I had overwhelmed myself somewhat, I never knew what I was in for.

I got lost, I was late to almost every class almost every day the first week.

Who knew there were so many kids in one town?!

Boys asked questions I had never heard of.

Did I want to go out with them? Was I a virgin? Had I ever kissed anyone?

Some girls acted like my best friend in one class but would laugh at me next class because they had more popular friends in it to talk to. Girls were also kind of mean as well, a lot of them would accuse me of liking their boyfriend when I wouldn't even know who he was.

The first few weeks were an emotional roller coaster resulting in tears at the end of almost every day.

I had nothing in common with these kids, I knew nothing of this world, of television, or artists, or really much about anything. I was new to this thing called life and kids could be so mean. I wanted to give up, but I didn't.

I was called slut, whore, fake, poor, pathetic, loser, liar, among other things, all in the first week.

Even though it was extremely hard, it was even more crazy and awesome to just talk to anyone I wanted without having to know what religion they were.

I was tough though, and I survived high school, not unscathed, but for the better. I made some of the most amazing friends a girl could have, to which I owe most of my sanity.

Thank you to those of you that showed me kindness and thank you to those that are still my friends.

Each of you showed me something different, and I remember something different about you all, and how you kindly responded to my awkward, weird and sheltered self. (Tiff, you deserve a whole chapter devoted to our adventures and amazing times, :) I could never find a better girl in the world to call my bestest friend! You absolutely rock!)

Friday, August 12, 2005, at 8:54 p.m. my sister had a beautiful baby girl! I was an aunt! I was so happy!

An aunt and a big sister all in the last year and twelve days! It's amazing how God works and the beautiful blessings he gives us!

24.

Mom and Galen had now been not getting along that well for months and months.

A loving, kind hearted man who had fallen to an addiction to alcohol through out his life, and he often showed a bad temper when a little too drunk. His bad temper could get out of hand, causing the house to hardly ever be quiet when they were both there. It was Mom and Dad all over again. The fighting the screaming, it was terrible.

I had grown to love Galen, he was like a father to me in many ways, but Mom didn't need this, not after all that she'd been through.

We left in 2006. I had a job, and I backed her fully. I had a car that Dad had bought for cheap and had me help him work on and fix up.
He then surprised me with giving it to me, so therefore I could work and go to school without needing a ride.
I borrowed Dad's truck for hauling things and Mom and I moved into town.

I was so proud of her, it takes so much courage to leave someone you love because they sometimes cannot break their bad habits and therefore treat you wrong in the long run; it can feel almost like it would be your fault if they made a bad choice when you left because you feel as if you left them in a bad spot, but you have to look out for yourself and you always have to follow where the Lord wants you to go.

Relationships like this with lovers, friends, family members, etc, can be so toxic to your life and state of mind.

These are times when you must deeply consider your heart and pray to God. Pray your heart out because you can't figure it out by yourself, you will try and you will fail without him.

One thing that never fails is love -
always continue to love but you must
love yourself too, and not in a vain "I
am beautiful and better than you" sort
of way but rather in a "I am capable of
ANYTHING through the Lord - he
gives me the strength to conquer any
and every situation I could EVER come
across" sort of way.

This self love and way of life will shine
and rub off and sometimes can help
more than you think.
Simple positivity is an amazing thing.

We decided a vacation was in order for

Mom and I. We went to Virginia Beach for a week. It was the most healing trip I've ever had. It was like all the years I'd not talked to her hadn't even happened.

That week helped my Mom too, we came home and settled back into life.

That summer was one of the best summers of my life. I made up for so much lost time with my Mom.
I love and respect her so much, she has endured so much more than any human should ever have to, having her children brainwashed and taken away, yet she kept her sanity.
She is an absolute hero to me and one

of the toughest, strongest, most caring
people I'l ever know.

25.

One day I was looking through a cabinet in the bookcase in the living room at Mom's when a book kind of just caught my eye.

Small, paperback, entitled "Life can be hard sometimes"
It was from Mom's step mother to Mom in 2000.

It's now 2007.

I halted….October…2000…Mom and

Dad started the divorce…I wonder if Mom ever wrote anything in here?

I flipped the papers, a lot of underling and highlighting, when the book fell open to the back pages.
My eyes were indulged immediately in the handwriting that spanned two whole pages.

It started…"Duane and The Lord's Farm"
As I read my eyes filled with tears at the pain and confusion in her words, but most of all what came through the lines was a mother's unwavering love:

"I am alone, hurting, scared, not

knowing if I'll see tomorrow because my pain feels too great, but what keeps me going is my good memories of Angel and Catie and knowing deep, deep inside that a time will come when they'll need me - I won't let you win!"

Every word got to me; knowing how much pain she'd suffered really hurt me.

Around the same time I was digging through my mother's Mom's photo albums and boxes of pictures and things one day and I came across some cards addressed to my sister and I from her that had been returned, unopened. We had been little, they were birthday cards. We obviously had been in the Lord's Farm at the time of sending.

I didn't need to ask, I could only imagine how heartbreaking it would be to have your child not allow you to see them or their children due to a cult. Not only to deny visits, but to return a birthday card as if you don't even exist anymore to them. The control one has to be under to think that is a Godly way of life is very evil indeed.

26.

When I was little, I let out anxieties by writing. I can write something I'll never ever say.
I often wrote out of anger, at the church, at God, at Dad and Mom, at everything that was happening.

When I moved in with Mom I took every single book and journal I'd ever wrote that I still had and burned them all, there was so much pain in them and confusion, I never wanted to read or even see them again.

As I wrote this book I could feel the coldness, resentment all over again, but nearing the finish of it, I am experiencing a different sort of emotion. I can feel the release of all of my life and thinking I would never be good enough for anything or anyone, I can feel day by day all of it slowly dissipating.

As if writing about my darkest days truly from the heart without coating any of it made the pain disperse, leaving in its place a sweet sense of release and calmness,innocence, gratitude.
The strength I had found was because of those dark days in your soul.
The days that are so beautiful to

everyone around you and it should be beautiful to you too, it's seventy degrees and the sun is shining, but it's not. All you see is blackness, death, pain, ripping, tearing at your heart deep inside, only you and God feel or know the pain is there.

Those days instilled in me a deep faith, a strength I would not have less the pain, and a fighting spirit.
I have found a calming place, the ability to put myself away from the situation and rest in the Lords arms.

I did not find this in the sermons at church or a book I read, I found this through suffering great pain and giving up and giving all to the Lord.

When you are at your lowest, and you're afraid you are going to fall in the black pit, what's worse..clinging on your own, slipping every minute, living in the fear that you are going to fall..or just saying "I'm gonna fall and God - I trust you to catch me" and just let go?

He will catch you, because he KNOWS you have nothing and no one left to trust, he wants you to let go, he WANTS you to trust him and to fall into his arms so he can carry your burden for you.

27.

It was fall time, the crisp clear air
smelled of apple cider, while sounds of
children laughing and playing fall on
your ears.
I was walking to the old hay barn,
where we had used to make cider.
This had been my favorite time of year
while we were in the church.

I stopped…looking around, things
seemed different, I seemed so much
older, and I didn't really recognize
anyone like I had known them, but I

knew who they all were.

I looked down at my hands, staring at my rings and bracelets. I recognized the rings immediately, one was from Mom the other from Ma.
I was confused, at the farm we didn't wear much jewelry, especially me! I never ever did.

Stopping dead in my tracks I turned and ran up to the farmhouse, through the front door and up the stairs. Bursting into the bathroom I looked into the mirror.
I looked the same, wearing a dress, tennis shoes, my hair was in a ponytail. This was me, the old, church me.

Frantically, I grabbed another mirror and held it behind my head, there it was, the last tattoo that I had gotten, in 2009.

"Angel!" I ran down the stairs screaming
"Where is my sister?!"
As I came around the porch outside I saw her.
Wait, she was getting into her car, her and her husbands Pontiac Vibe.
"Angel! Stop! Wait for me!" I yelled loud.
She turned, a twisted look on her face.

"Why in the world are you yelling? What's wrong with you?" She asked, seeming truly puzzled.

My heart sank.

"Angel! What's wrong with YOU?! Why are we back here??"

"What do you mean Catie?….Are you ok?"

"Where is Mom?! Don't you know whose car you're getting into? Where's your two children?"

"Ummm…aww….Catie…no….you poor thing…please don't make…don't you remember??? We haven't seen Mom since you were old enough to stay home from visitation, and this is Joan's car she wants me to run real quick for milk; you wanna go?"

"ANGEL!" I grabbed her, by now I was shaking, maybe even harder than I was shaking her - I snapped my fingers in front of her face.

"Angel! You have two kids! You're married! I live at our Grandma's - I have a job I graduated high school - Mom, we see her like every day - she's remarried to-"
She cut me off
"Catie! Stop it! You're being....CRAZY!!"

"NO IM NOT!!" I was still screaming so loud.

"Just get in! Trust me! I'll prove it to you!" I shouted.

We got in the car and drove down the driveway towards Gorman Lane.
When we got to the gate I got out to unlock the combination lock…
1..9..1..2..
I tried it three different times, it wouldn't open.
Angel got out, put in a different combination, the lock opened.
"Don't you remember? We changed the locks since Mom?" She asked.

"ANGEL! THIS IS NOT OUR LIFE ANYMORE!" I was in tears - how could this happen? How could she not remember?

"Catie, get in the car we have to get milk"

"NO! THIS IS NOT WHO WE ARE!" I hit the ground, screaming, crying.

"WHY! HOW??? Was I really living this nightmare?? Where did our new lives go??? Did I just imagine the past eight years??

"PLEASE GOD! I DONT KNOW IF I CAN HANDLE THIS! WHAT IS HAPPENING?"

I was screaming, trying to breathe.

I was beating my fists off the ground, on my knees, face down on my legs, Angel was pulling, trying to get me up off the dirt and gravel….

….I sat up, my eyes flew open, I was still beating my fists, still crying, a pink square was making noise - I grabbed it, running down the stairs and out the back door.

It was 4-28-2010, the sky was beautiful, spring blossoms everywhere, the birds were singing, the sun was shining..
I realized it had been a dream, the pink square turned out to be my cell phone…

I hit the ground once again on my knees, my face bowed to the Lord, thanking him, emotions spilling out of me, thanking him for his mercy, allowing it to just be a dream, for allowing reality to be real.

It made me realize how much I had changed, how thankful I was for my life as it is.
For having my family back, freedom, the ability to wear, do, say what I want, be friends with who I wanted, talk to anyone I wanted, have a job, fall in love - freedom to live.
One never realizes how seemingly little luxuries such as these are all too often taken for granted...

Peace I leave with you, my peace, not the worlds peace but mine, let not your

heart be troubled, neither let it be afraid
- John 14:27

somehow I've lost my way

the path seemed much clearer

in the light of day

as the night goes on..it only gets darker

somewhere I've lost myself

not sure where to pick up

hiding behind the smile

if you could just spend a while

inside my head

you would know what I meant

when I said

I don't know where I went

never been here before

the sun is gone

the weight of the world is crushing

even more

the clouds have rolled in

I don't know if I can handle much more

but before I give up let me stop
to count my blessings and I realize
my cup is overflowing
pouring over the top
and I see the world
through much clearer eyes
-Catie Cartwright

28.

When I started working at Rocky Gap after graduating high school I'll never forget the woman doing my interview told me not to play with my hair during an interview. I was nervous, I really wanted a good job and this looked really good to me.

The team of ladies (and a few housemen) that I joined were headstrong, independent, and loads of fun.

Here was me, little Catie, at a real job with real people from all walks of life.

These women taught me so much about life. How to put on the face that was customer service no matter what they were going through.

How to look prepared at five a.m., How to deal with rude people and not become a rude person yourself.

How to be a woman, a respectable woman with values that works hard and plays even harder.

I laughed and cried with these women. They became like family to me.

I'll always have a special place in my heart for those original girls I met in banquets that helped me to have the voice that I have today.

They taught me in a different way than my Mother that I had the right to say how I would be treated in all aspects of life.

This combined with my Mother's good morals and principals helped me be able to say I am grateful for the woman that I have become.

Thank you banquet girls, you all never knew how much I was listening and learning from our conversations and laughter.
Each one of you contribute to a link of my back bone I never knew I had

before I met you.

29.

The memory of being told by Joan that
day that I didn't have any family
outside of the church, and that they
were my family now has vividly stayed
with me through out the years.
I never forgot the look in her eyes when
she said that.

Eyes are truly the window to the soul,
they say what words may never.

Instantly I felt as though I had done
something wrong, by speaking of
someone who had been my loving Pap,

but who was now supposed to be no one to me?

How could my family just not be my family anymore? I didn't really understand that, and now I see, its because it was wrong.
Of course I didn't understand them.

During the beginning of Mom getting sick and thrown out of her home and church, the locks were literally changed at the house and the farm so she couldn't get back in.

One day, Dad, Angel and I returned home in the evening from the farm. It had been a usual day it seemed, but days down there were so busy half of the time I didn't know who was there and who wasn't.

I don't remember who was there that day and who wasn't. Anyway, we arrived home and our house was trashed.

Things were dumped out, knocked over, it looked like we had been robbed.
We were told that Mom had been there and made that horrible mess, and taken all sorts of things.

I would have been really mad if I had been her, and I knew that when I was little, so I didn't question this at all. I also actually understood something for once.

I always heard Mom deny this (in court, etc) but I never personally talked with her about this.

Fast forward approximately seventeen years from when that happened, we are at my Pap's house for Christmas and we are watching a home video of him catching and trapping all sorts of cool animals.

Then the video ends, and I can see he was taping over an old home video.

The first image on the screen is of this little heart shelf with a little blue cow on it on the top of the landing at our house in Greenspring. The video begins to pan left to include the living room-

Pap jumps up and turns the video off.
I jump up.
"WHAT WAS THAT?!?" I ask.

So we watch, and we see Mom leave our house in Greenspring with items that were only hers such as clothing etc, and the house was left in perfect condition, nothing out of place.

How had it been so easy for them to lie to me? To destroy my home and things

and tell me my own mother did it?!?

To set her up like that? Pure evil!
I confronted my Father about this and
he had been at work all day, he only
remembers coming home to a mess and
being told it was Mom that did it.

I also confronted my Dad in recent
years about the trailer full of mine and
my sister's items.

What was on that trailer was all
material things, yes, but they were
rightfully ours.
Everything we ever had was on that
trailer except for the few clothes we

kept and the few items I had hidden away.

Not me, Mom, nor my sister went through anything that went on that trailer.
Our Father was told it had all been gone through and it was things that my sister and I did not want, so he could get rid of it all, and he did just that.

This, obviously, was a LIE.
Every book I had, from the Little Pilgrim's Progress to my Dr Seuss collection was gone, yet somehow, a series of books Haley had given me survived.

30.

When my great grandmother died, as I wrote earlier, I wasn't allowed to go to the funeral or anything.
I had not even seen her in years, I wasn't allowed to visit her, I missed her so bad.

Sadly, I wasn't with her when she died, but my heart was, and years later, I came across an old birthday card from her to me that was returned to her from us when we had been in the cult.
In her broken, shaky handwriting she had scribbled "love ya, ma."

I had the dates of her birth and death, and her signature tattooed on me. When Haley saw this she commented on how much of a waste of time a tattoo is.

Honestly, I don't think anyone has a right to tell another what a waste of their time is or not, you are the ruler of your own life.
The fact that I can get a tattoo on me, and no one can simply take it away is very sacred to me.
I have several of them, and they all have a very special meaning to me.
Perhaps it is a bit materialistic, but something about being able to see them

and remember their meaning no matter when it is or where I am does a lot to keep me grounded.
In essence, my ink is not only art, but in every way can be connected to something deep inside of me.
A belief, a promise, a memory, a loss, a gain, a new life.
Unfortunately I don't have a lot of memories of my Uncle Keese, however the ones I do have are amazing.
My uncle was truly a radiant soul, more full of life than most of the world, and always ready to make you smile.

I know that he would be proud of me for finishing this book, and I'm certain that he is smiling down on me as I write this.

One day I will have a tattoo in his memory as well.

31.

As one gets older, usually life has a way of showing things. The older I get the more I find out, wether through life, or just by asking people, because, believe it or not, asking wasn't something to be done.
That was considered backsliding, not doing well, etc.

So many people have not a clue as to the real weight and feel of the fear associated with mind control and cult behaviors.
The results of questions asked by adults are far too severe for a child to even consider asking questions.

Real fear is when you are taught that you are going to hell with no more chances for forgiveness left for doing something the cult considers "not of God."

In a cult this can mean perhaps resisting a leader or leading member on a subject as seemingly simple as a cake mix, or as important as a new job or home.

Real fear is when you are brainwashed by someone so manipulative that they use the guise of being a protective leader, someone who cares about you and your family's well being, to gain your utmost trust, only to literally tear your life apart and crumble your sanity.

You are on constant eggshells, there is
no clear line on what may or may not
send you to hell.
There is no having negative emotions
or feelings.

Everything is an act to receive
assurance of being safe from getting
thrown out, losing your family, never
being allowed back, and burning in hell
forever for not acting like a perfect,
happy, always smiling, never upset no
matter what (did I mention perfect?)
shell of a person.

I never asked questions, I didn't ask

how or why, I simply believed what I had been taught from the tender young age of two.

Asking nothing results in no answers, and a blinded way of life. You allow another to decide what is best for you, and when and where.
This often results in confusion, depression, and high levels of anxiety.

These symptoms are often overlooked by the managing of them in a child's brain. When a child experiences traumatic events, often the brain will react in a way to protect the child.
This can happen as an adult also, however I have first hand experience as

a child.

The brain tends to suppress events as a way to get past them. Certain events and memories will disappear to a dark, not often visited domain. Along with these go the reactions and emotions the child felt.
They are hidden and un dealt with, unacknowledged and locked away.

Until you reach a level of security and spiritual growth where you can say to yourself that you were wronged and acknowledge it, many times these emotional scars are left seeping emotional issues.

Since no one ever told you "Hey! You were wronged, I'm sorry, or hey this was wrong, that wasn't fair to happen to you!"
You probably never felt you had the right to think about it or dwell on it to even process it. That is how I felt.

I've come to find we all have our own path to healing after trauma, and that no ones is easy.

No matter what you go through, remember to take time, acknowledge the event, scream, cry, grieve, write. Allow yourself the time to do this to help you heal.

32.

When I was starting ninth grade I really should have been in some sort of therapy that would have helped prepare me at least some for the culture shock I was in for.

Imagine taking Laura from Little House on the Prairie and dropping her into 2014.
People can be so mean sometimes, and they have no clue what you have been through.

What is so unfortunate for ex cult members, especially for people who grew up in a cult, is that there are no specific groups or therapists that deal with this sort of thing. Not many people are educated on cult awareness.

There are no pamphlets for things like, how to join society, or warning you about cults and the warning signs.

A major red flag that a group is a cult is when one or two people are clearly the leaders and the others literally have no voice of their own.

Our government has created the perfect breeding grounds for religious evil by overlooking loopholes in the system. These loopholes destroy families, children, and make things that should be illegal legal.

Our children's lives, spiritual and physical are at stake when it comes to these things being changed. We need a system that responds to religious abuse as harshly as the abuse is felt.

33.

To finish this book completely I took a
backpacking trip (short) maybe six or
eight miles, not positive. I took myself
and my dog, and went to a very
secluded trail (we saw five people all
day) hiked for about three hours
through some beautiful West Virginia
backwoods to an amazing little
campsite beside a creek.

I laid out my sittin' blanket, pulled off
my socks and shoes and began to write.
I sat here for probably two hours, not
one person went by, such solitude,
serenity.

We ate a lunch of jerky, peanut butter sandwiches, packed up and hiked two and a half hours to this beautiful set of maples with low hanging branches.

Here we sat for maybe four hours as I continued to finish up my writing.
I thank God for times like this.
I am my most at home, alone in the woods.
As a kid, everything made the most sense in the woods, and it still seems to for me today.

I don't build forts as much as I used to, or climb trees as often, but I do spend as much of my time outside as possible.

If you have never taken a solo hike for longer than three hours, do yourself a favor and try it.

Being in nature recharges the inner soul, releases your mind of needless thoughts and cares, to only what is in front of you.
A lot of stress can release from exerting energy hiking, while the mind clears from the peace of nature. All the while the soul is being rejuvenated.

34.

demoralizing and demeaning
all of your evil ways
you're a monster
this is your own game
laughing in my face
spitting your degrading words
demented beliefs meant to shame
me to thinking I was disgraced
you will pay the price
for all your deceptive lies
consumed childhood's innocence
destroyed family ties
never thought for a moment
of the torment your acts would cause

instead you called yourself sanctified
while terrorizing and brainwashing
those you 'loved'
not only me cut off from the world
yet still isolated and alone instead
at least I had a friend to turn to
and he will judge you the last night you
rest your vile head
-Catie Cartwright

I am no longer ashamed
of who I have become
of the experiences that I've lived that created
for me the Battle of a childhood
sequestered and numb

no longer do I feel weak
for the hurt that I have gone through
I finally found my voice
after the years my strength is new
my heart no longer aches to speak

I am all that I am
because through great pain
I learned to stand on my own
I didn't need to hold your hand
through weakness I became strong

I am a survivor
my scars reveal the wars I have fought
never again will I be silenced
because now I am stronger
no longer a victim,
I am a warrior
-Catie Cartwright

35.

"Pure religion and undefiled is
"ministering unto," not the other thing,
"being ministered unto."
It is handing over the morning paper to
another for first perusal.
It is vacating a pleasant seat by the fire
for the one who comes in chilled.
It is giving the most restful arm chair or
sofa corner for one who is weary. It is
'moving up' in the pew to let the new
comer sit down by the entrance.
It is rising to darken the blind when the
suns rays shine in too brightly upon
some face in the circle.

It is giving up your comfort and convenience very time for the comfort and convenience of another.

This is at once true courtesy and christianity."

- rev A.L.Stone

"In essence, true christianity is, simply, love."

-Catie Cartwright

To those of you that feel like there's never an end, possibly never even a reason, never knowing when they are going to break, just remember that out of pain comes strength and there's a reason for the pain.

Just as a storm comes before a rainbow, heartache and pain must come before we can openly exhibit our true colors.

While we may be confused and hurting, let our minds and hearts be strong, confident in knowing that we will one day shine brighter than the stars.

This is the end of my story…..For now….What will yours be?

~ The End ~